A POEM OF HER OWN

VOICES OF AMERICAN WOMEN YESTERDAY AND TODAY

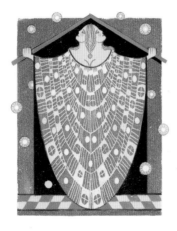

EDITED BY
Catherine Clinton

ILLUSTRATED BY
Stephen Alcorn

HARRY N. ABRAMS, INC., PUBLISHERS

CONTENTS

INTRODUCTION

=◦➧○❋○➧◦=

Poetry was born within American women, even before there was a nation known as the United States. Women were the keepers of the culture, the voices which sang out, the poetic imaginations unleashed within what would be called "the New World." Certainly women who landed on North America's shores from Europe and Africa—and eventually from Asia and Central and South America—brought with them the rhythms and languages of their diverse cultures. Native American women whose ancestors had long before occupied the continent had distinctive offerings as well.

Over time, women in America found creative outlets though verse, expressing themselves with the power of words. Some, like African-born Phillis Wheatley, became internationally celebrated within their own lifetimes. Others, like Emily Dickinson, only found a wide audience after they died, through publication of their work posthumously. But hundreds of women poets left us a rich treasure trove—creating poems of their own, poems for us to find and appreciate, poems for us to memorize and cherish. This bounty remains a vital contribution to our national literature.

It would be impossible to fill a single volume with the work of all American women who have published wonderful poetry. Even the best poets present too many choices. But the following selection captures a range of voices which together are meant to breathe life into American women's poetry.

The poems are listed in chronological order to showcase women's poetic voices as they appeared within the past, while capsule biographies of the twenty-five women poets are listed alphabetically and found at the back of the book. These brief sketches of women poets reveal not only individuals, but, together, comprise a particularly intriguing story of America, a story of courage in the face of hardship, a story which traces varieties of creative expression unfolding over three centuries.

It is only fitting that the first American poet published in English was a woman. Like many wives who sailed to European colonies, Anne Bradstreet was considered a helpmeet for her husband, a valuable asset to her household, but not expected to do much beyond tending her hearth and garden. The British-born Bradstreet had been an apt pupil during her early years in Lincolnshire, England, and found exile on the hardscrabble New England frontier frustrating. She channeled her emotional and intellectual energies into writing, scribbling verses on precious linen by the flickering firelight. She let domestic obligations such as children and housework become inspiration for her poems. Bradstreet plaintively asked her colonial readers: "Who says my hand a needle better fits?" and answered with stirring poems which awakened admirers on both sides of the Atlantic. Yet her question still rings true for us today.

And what of the enslaved Phillis Wheatley, whose polished sonnets proved that neither bondage, nor color, nor gender are necessarily obstacles to literary accomplishment? If Wheatley could earn fame and praise, why should she and fellow Africans remain enslaved? This was a question that most white colonists, struggling with their own Revolution, hoped to avoid.

Wheatley, sold on the auction block in Boston when just a young girl, was forced to prove herself again and again to doubters who questioned her abilities. Even such strong champions of Wheatley's talents as Thomas Paine and Benjamin Franklin were unable to protect her from prejudice. Wheatley struggled against traditional attitudes that women and blacks must remain "in their place," a place where opportunity dared not enter, where equality was barred. Her talents had impressed lords and ladies on a visit to England and George

Washington complimented her on her prose, yet Wheatley's early success faded and she died impoverished and forgotten. It would be several generations before her reputation as a significant poet would be revived.

The War for Independence ended with the birth of a new nation. When the American republic was in its infancy, changes rapidly transformed roles for men and women, black and white, native and immigrant. Calls for liberty and equality rippled across the countryside, challenging the first generation of American poets to rise to the occasion.

Several distinctive women's voices joined the chorus. In what other country would the orphaned daughter of a sea captain, forced into factory labor as an eleven-year-old girl, go on to become a writer, educator, and poet of note? Surely the poetry of former mill girl Lucy Larcom exemplified the flowering of American democracy.

The contrast of voices—Emily Dickinson (guarded and private) and Julia Ward Howe (extremely public)—demonstrates the two extremes of women writers during America's early years. While the Belle of Amherst (as Dickinson was known) stayed hidden away in her bedroom, sewing her poems into secret folios tucked away in drawers, Julia Ward Howe mounted the platform to champion the Union Cause during the Civil War. Her "Battle-Hymn of the Republic" remains one of the most celebrated verses by any American woman.

When today we sing "Over the River and Through the Woods," few of us recall the words were written by abolitionist Lydia Maria Child. President Lincoln declared Thanksgiving a national holiday during the Civil War. And so Child created this poem of celebration ("Hurrah for the pumpkin pie!") during a dark time in our nation's history. Both the Thanksgiving poem and the "Battle-Hymn of the Republic" were poetry set to music. The enduring popularity of these songs remind us that verses can often live on when set to music, and reach a wider audience than the average poem.

Certainly, many Americans can recite by heart the lines—"Give me your tired, your poor, your huddled masses yearning to breathe free . . . ." But few remember the name of the poem ("The New Colossus") or the name of the poet (Emma Lazarus). These words are carved into the base of the Statue of Liberty to remind us that we are a nation of immigrants, a refuge for exiles from around the globe.

Migrations have shaped our nation. Certainly the movement of African-Americans out of the South and into the North at the turn of the twentieth century was a landmark event. Alice Dunbar-Nelson, like other black poets of her generation, wrote about the topic of oppression. She was a member of the generation that witnessed America's participation in what was at first "the Great War," but later became known as World War I, a battle Americans joined in 1917.

A larger number of American women poets carved out space for themselves within American literary circles following World War I. During the 1920s, notable women poets were mainly college educated—and the best of them purposely sought to make a mark in the world of poetry. Marianne Moore edited an influential New York magazine, *The Dial*. She was much beloved by the male poets of her Greenwich Village circle, and dubbed "Our Saint" by fellow poets. Equally beloved, but with a much less saintly reputation, Edna St. Vincent Millay was not only one of the most famous poets of her day (the first woman to earn the Pulitzer Prize for Poetry), but her verse celebrated her bohemian lifestyle. She was both romantic and unconventional in her choice of friends and lovers, and described herself as "burning the candle at both ends."

Unfortunately, this first new generation of women poets who gained a foothold in the predominantly male literary world found they paid a high price for their struggles to break down the barricades. Indeed, several of these female poets (Bogan, Sexton, and Plath) battled against mental illness throughout most of their adult lives. Fellow poet W.H. Auden commended his friend Louise Bogan for the "unflinching courage with which she faced her problems, her determination never to surrender to self-pity, but to wrest beauty and joy out of dark places."

Anne Sexton actually turned to poetry as a form of therapy, a therapy which launched her brilliant career as a writer and teacher, but one that did not save her from suicide. Sylvia Plath also took her own life, failing to write her way out of a period of bleak despair in 1963. Dead at thirty-one, Plath left behind scores of unpublished verses and most of her poems were published posthumously.

Many other twentieth-century women poets found writing poetry life-affirming. Despite youthful reversals in love and career plans, Gertrude Stein delved deep within herself and discovered a rich vein of creative talent and cultivated a powerful literary voice. She became one of the most prolific writers of her day and one of the best-known experimental poets during her own lifetime. Stein spent most of her life abroad, yet was a distinctively American writer whose verses—most famously "a rose is a rose is a rose"—played with language. This playfulness perhaps masked Stein's extremely serious commitment to change the face of American literature. Stein's literary generation flourished between America's participation in the two World Wars [World War I (1917–19) and World War II (1941–45)]. These modern poets not only used verse as a form of self-expression, but they wanted their poetry to offer political insight, perhaps even to serve as a vehicle of protest.

Dissenting and radical poets have made their mark in modern American verse. At times, the "personal" and "the political" fused together. Sometimes seamlessly, as in the case of African-American poet Gwendolyn Brooks. This talented black writer spent much of her life on Chicago's South Side where she was a keen observer of inner city life. Brooks's poems were snapshots of everyday routine. Although she wrote about and within the confines of a single urban setting, her voice has universal appeal. Brooks's second poetry collection earned her the Pulitzer Prize, the first ever awarded to an African-American.

By the last decades of the twentieth century, many women poets broke with male literary tradition, and some wrote poems focusing on their womanhood. These new feminist voices were poets such as Anne Sexton, who wanted to "sing in celebration of the woman I am." Her intense, confessional style confronted readers with a poet's most riveting observations on both sex and sexism (discrimination on the basis of gender). She stimulated a blossoming of feminist creative expression, which included Marge Piercy and Adrienne Rich, among others. Rich suggested, "Long before I could write as a lesbian I was writing as a woman, in a period when to do so was believed to opt for the non-universal, the minor, even the trivial."

Women poets struggled to negotiate a path through the thicket of late twentieth-century American culture, to come into their own. Some, like African-American poets Nikki Giovanni and Lucille Clifton, celebrate both femaleness and blackness within many of their works. Clifton explored her African roots and women ancestors, quiltmakers and storytellers, who shaped her voice. Poets like Sandra Cisneros and Julia Alvarez draw on Hispanic girlhoods to create vibrant, dynamic images of coming of age. Hawaiian-born poet Cathy Song, inspired by the stories of her grandmother's generation, offers us images of picture brides who crossed the Pacific to marry men who had selected them from their photographs. She wove her own grandmother's story into her inspiring poetry, as did Naomi Shihab Nye. Nye's Palestinian grandmother on her father's side and her German grandmother on her mother's side filled young Naomi with family lore. This created within her a deep love of stories, shining through in Nye's compelling poetic testimony to the immigrant experience. As pathbreakers, representing both their gender and their ethnic or racial heritage, these poets who spring from more diverse cultures have broadened and deepened American literature.

Modern American poetry has been immeasurably enriched by the contributions of Native American writers as well. American Indian women have too often been barely visible in traditional history, and romanticized objects in American literature. So the emergence of voices of Native American women has been a powerful literary development. Leslie Marmon Silko has confided that much of her poetry springs from the Navajo stories of her childhood. Her New Mexican girlhood inspired early verses, a body of work with vision and imagination at its core.

Vision and imagination are not only essential to creating poetry, but also perhaps the key to appreciating poetry. Many of the poets in this volume started out as teachers or became teachers, perhaps as an outgrowth of twin talents as nurturers and creators. In the nineteenth century, Lucy Larcom dedicated her talents both to students and young readers. Larcom's poems were mainly drawn from her own abbreviated New England girlhood—idyllic years before her father died and before she was sent to work in the mills. She conjured up nostalgia with poems full of the beauty of nature and the sweetness of days gone by.

This theme of a lost world of nature and nostalgia echoes from the sable curtains of night in Phillis Wheatley's "An Hymn to the Evening" to the snowy banks in Lydia Maria Child's

Thanksgiving song to the juniper woods of Leslie Marmon Silko's "In Cold Storm Light" to the exotic pumpkins along Marge Piercy's "A Road Through the Woods." Images of the lost worlds of girlhood also echo in the verses of countless American women poets, reflected in Adrienne Rich's "Bears," Sandra Cisneros's "Good Hotdogs," and Nikki Giovanni's "Girls in the Circle."

One of the recurrent subjects treated in American women's poetry is the theme of family. From the earliest American poetry of Anne Bradstreet to the newest work by Julia Alvarez, mothers, fathers, and siblings crowd into verses. There are extended families in the bustling Chicago tenements of Gwendolyn Brooks's poetry and in the distant mountain villages in Cathy Song's verses. There are babies in Sylvia Plath's poems and grandmothers in Naomi Shihab Nye's verses—generations which enfold and can even engulf the poet's creative imagination. In some of their richest work, women poets include families they know and love, families they never knew and miss, families they hope to build, and sometimes even families they wish to escape.

Although women consistently confront issues of hearth and home, women poets also seek subjects exploring the wider world. This examination of public, political issues in women's poetry has met with mixed results. Before the Civil War, women poets like Lydia Maria Child

were scorned for expressing dissenting political views—even ostracized. Less than a hundred years later, Edna St. Vincent Millay was applauded when she publicly condemned the execution of Sacco and Vanzetti in 1927. During a time of political hysteria and "xenophobia" (fear of foreigners), these two Italian immigrants were convicted of murder on what was believed by their sympathizers to be insufficient evidence. Writers across the nation, women poets included, used their voices to protest injustice and to stir up support for dissenting causes. Poets could use their words and their fame to stir passions.

A rising tide of radical protest has influenced American women's poetry during the past half century. Poets represented in this volume, such as Nikki Giovanni, Marge Piercy, and Adrienne Rich have all used their art to support a variety of political causes, and to express political dissent. Rich even refused the National

Medal of Arts to protest government policy in 1997. These outspoken women poets have been at the forefront of movements for peace and justice.

Finally, it is no surprise that women poets have frequently confronted issues about being women—revealed in such provocative pieces as Louise Bogan's "Women," Edna St. Vincent Millay's "[I, being born a woman and distressed]," Anne Sexton's "Her Kind," and Mary Jo Salter's "What Do Women Want?" Many of the most memorable verses explore the tribulations women face with female stereotyping, such as Lucille Clifton's sassy "Homage to My Hips" and Alice Dunbar-Nelson's wrenching "I Sit and Sew." Some poets use irony, while others use humor—and still others employ both to attack prejudice and put-downs.

Women poets proudly possess, as Sandra Cisneros proclaims, "the magic of words." When they employ their literary charms to cast a spell, they empower women—whatever their race or class or background or age. But these poems are not for women only. They serve a global purpose as well. Appreciation of one another's poetry, Naomi Shihab Nye suggests, humanizes us and offers hope that we might find a way to live together.

The women poets which follow only have one thing in common: they can enhance and enrich us as readers, if we let them. Some, like Dickinson and Plath, may have failed to connect with a mass audience during their own lifetimes. Yet with their inspiring work, they left behind pieces of themselves and these poems to let us peek inside their intense, creative imaginations.

For poets living and dead, we must do our best to listen to their voices. If we try, we can hear as well as see their words on the page—we can feel as well as read the verses which follow. *A Poem of Her Own* shows the magic of words. This remains a gift from the poets to us— a gift that we can open page by page. ❧

— CATHERINE CLINTON

THE AUTHOR TO HER BOOK

ANNE BRADSTREET

Thou ill-formed offspring of my feeble brain,
Who after birth didst by my side remain,
Till snatched from thence by friends, less wise than true,
Who thee abroad, exposed to public view,
Made thee in rags, halting to th' press to trudge,
Where errors were not lessened (all may judge).
At thy return my blushing was not small,
My rambling brat (in print) should mother call,
I cast thee by as one unfit for light,
Thy visage was so irksome in my sight;
Yet being mine own, at length affection would
Thy blemishes amend, if so I could:
I washed thy face, but more defects I saw,
And rubbing off a spot still made a flaw.
I stretched thy joints to make thee even feet,
Yet still thou run'st more hobbling than is meet;
In better dress to trim thee was my mind,
But nought save homespun cloth i' th' house I find.
In this array 'mongst vulgars may'st thou roam.
In critic's hands beware thou dost not come,
And take thy way where yet thou art not known
If for thy father asked, say thou hadst none;
And for thy mother, she alas is poor,
Which caused her thus to send thee out of door.

1678

AN HYMN TO THE EVENING
PHILLIS WHEATLEY

Soon as the sun forsook the eastern main
The pealing thunder shook the heav'nly plain;
Majestic grandeur! From the zephyr's wing,
Exhales the incense of the blooming spring.
Soft purl the streams, the birds renew their notes,
And through the air their mingled music floats.

Through all the heav'ns what beauteous dyes are
    spread!
But the west glories in the deepest red:
So may our breasts with ev'ry virtue glow,
The living temples of our God below!

Fill'd with the praise of him who gives the light,
And draws the sable curtains of the night,
Let placid slumbers soothe each weary mind,
At morn to wake more heav'nly, more refin'd;

So shall the labors of the day begin
More pure, more guarded from the snares of sin.

Night's leaden sceptre seals my drowsy eyes,
Then cease, my song, till fair Aurora rise.

1773

THE BROWN THRUSH

LUCY LARCOM

There's a merry brown thrush sitting up in the tree;
'He's singing to me! he's singing to me!'
And what does he say, little girl, little boy?
'Oh, the world's running over with joy!
　　Don't you hear? Don't you see?
　　Hush! look! in my tree!
　　I'm as happy as happy can be!'

And the brown thrush keeps singing, 'A nest do you see,
And five eggs hid by me in the juniper-tree?
Don't meddle! don't touch! little girl, little boy,
　　Now I'm glad! now I'm free!
　　And I always shall be,
　　If you never bring sorrow to me.'

So the merry brown thrush sings away in the tree,
To you and to me, to you and to me;
And he sings all the day, little girl, little boy,
'Oh, the world's running over with joy!
　　But long it won't be,
　　Don't you know? don't you see?
　　Unless we are as good as can be!'

DATE UNKNOWN

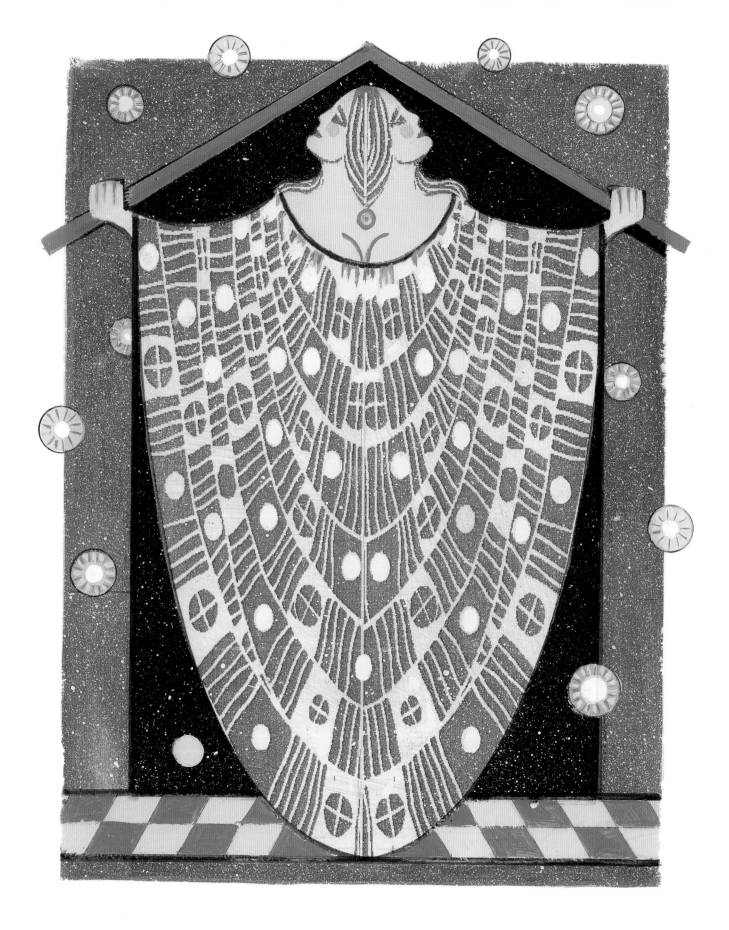

657

EMILY DICKINSON

I dwell in Possibility—
A fairer House than Prose—
More numerous of Windows—
Superior—for Doors—

Of Chambers as the Cedars—
Impregnable of Eye—
And for an Everlasting Roof
The Gambrels of the Sky—

Of Visitors—the fairest—
For Occupation—This—
The spreading wide my narrow Hands
The gather Paradise—

DATE UNKNOWN

THE BATTLE-HYMN OF THE REPUBLIC

JULIA WARD HOWE

Mine eyes have seen the glory of the coming of the Lord:

He is trampling out the vintage where the grapes of wrath are stored;

He hath loosed the fateful lightning of his terrible swift sword:

    His truth is marching on.

I have seen him in the watch-fires of a hundred circling camps;

They have builded him an altar in the evening dews and damps;

I can read his righteous sentence by the dim and flaring lamps:

    His day is marching on.

I have read a fiery gospel, writ in burnished rows of steel:

"As ye deal with my contemners, so with you my grace shall deal;

Let the Hero, born of woman, crush the serpent with his heel,

    Since God is marching on."

He has sounded forth the trumpet that shall never call retreat;

He is sifting out the hearts of men before his judgment-seat:

O, be swift, my soul, to answer him! Be jubilant, my feet!

    Our God is marching on.

In the beauty of the lilies Christ was born across the sea,

With a glory in his bosom that transfigures you and me;

As he died to make men holy, let us die to make men free,

    While God is marching on.

1862

THE NEW-ENGLAND BOY'S SONG
ABOUT THANKSGIVING DAY

LYDIA MARIA CHILD

Over the river, and through the wood,
  To grandfather's house we go;
    The horse knows the way,
    To carry the sleigh,
  Through the white and drifted snow.

Over the river, and through the wood,
  To grandfather's house away!
    We would not stop
    For doll or top,
  For 't is Thanksgiving day.

Over the river, and through the wood,
  Oh, how the wind does blow!
    It stings the toes,
    And bites the nose,
  As over the ground we go.

Over the river, and through the wood,
  With a clear blue winter sky,
    The dogs do bark,
    And children hark,
  As we go jingling by.

Over the river, and through the wood,
  To have a first-rate play—
    Hear the bells ring
    Ting a ling ding,
  Hurra for Thanksgiving day!

Over the river, and through the wood—
    No matter for winds that blow;
        Or if we get
        The sleigh upset,
    Into a bank of snow.

Over the river, and through the wood,
    To see little John and Ann;
        We will kiss them all,
        And play snow-ball,
    And stay as long as we can.

Over the river, and through the wood,
    Trot fast, my dapple grey!
        Spring over the ground,
        Like a hunting hound,
    For 't is Thanksgiving day!

Over the river, and through the wood,
    And straight through the barn-yard gate;
        We seem to go
        Extremely slow,
    It is so hard to wait.

Over the river, and through the wood—
    Old Jowler hears our bells;
        He shakes his pow,
        With a loud bow wow,
    And thus the news he tells.

Over the river, and through the wood—
  When grandmother sees us come,
    She will say, Oh dear,
     The children are here,
  Bring pie for every one.

Over the river, and through the wood—
  Now grandmother's cap I spy!
    Hurra for the fun!
    Is the pudding done?
  Hurra for the pumpkin pie!

CIRCA 1863

THE NEW COLOSSUS

EMMA LAZARUS

Not like the brazen giant of Greek fame,
With conquering limbs astride from land to land;
Here at our sea-washed, sunset gates shall stand
A mighty woman with a torch, whose flame
Is the imprisoned lightning, and her name
Mother of Exiles, From her beacon-hand
Glows world-wide welcome; her mild eyes command
The air-bridged harbor that twin cities frame.
"Keep, ancient lands, your storied pomp!" cries she
With silent lips. "Give me your tired, your poor,
Your huddled masses yearning to breathe free,
The wretched refuse of your teeming shore.
Send these, the homeless, tempest-tost to me,
I lift my lamp beside the golden door!"

1888

I SIT AND SEW

ALICE DUNBAR-NELSON

I sit and sew—a useless task it seems,
My hands grown tired, my head weighed down with dreams—
The panoply of war, the martial tread of men,
Grim-faced, stern-eyed, gazing beyond the ken
Of lesser souls, whose eyes have not seen Death
Nor learned to hold their lives but as a breath—
But—I must sit and sew.

I sit and sew—my heart aches with desire—
That pageant terrible, that fiercely pouring fire
On wasted fields, and writing grotesque things
Once men. My soul in pity flings
Appealing cries, yearning only to go
There in that holocaust of hell, those fields of woe—
But—I must sit and sew.

The little useless seam, the idle patch;
Why dream I here beneath my homely thatch,
When there they lie in sodden mud and rain,
Pitifully calling me, the quick ones and the slain?
You need me, Christ! It is no roseate dream
That beckons me—this pretty futile seam,
It stifles me—God, must I sit and sew?

1920

POETRY

MARIANNE MOORE

I, too, dislike it: there are things that are important beyond all
    this fiddle.
  Reading it, however, with a perfect contempt for it, one
    discovers in
it after all, a place for the genuine.
    Hands that can grasp, eyes
     that can dilate, hair that can rise
      if it must, these things are important not because a

high-sounding interpretation can be put upon them but because
    they are
useful. When they become so derivative as to become
    unintelligible,
the same thing may be said for all of us, that we
    do not admire what
    we cannot understand: the bat
     holding on upside down or in quest of something to

eat, elephants pushing, a wild horse taking a roll, a tireless
    wolf under a tree, the immovable critic twitching his skin
    like a horse that feels a flea, the base-
ball fan, the statistician—
  nor is it valid
    to discriminate against 'business documents and

school-books'; all these phenomena are important. One must
        make a distinction
    however: when dragged into prominence by half poets, the
        result is not poetry,
  nor till the poets among us can be
      'literalists of
        the imagination,—above
          insolence and triviality and can present

for inspection, imaginary gardens with real toads in them, shall
        we have
    it. In the meantime, if you demand on the one hand,
    the raw material of poetry in
      all its rawness and
      that which is on the other hand
          genuine, then you are interested in poetry.

1921

[I, BEING BORN A WOMAN AND DISTRESSED]

EDNA ST. VINCENT MILLAY

I, being born a woman and distressed

By all the needs and notions of my kind,

Am urged by your propinquity to find

Your person fair, and feel a certain zest

To bear your body's weight upon my breast:

So subtly is the fume of life designed,

To clarify the pulse and cloud the mind,

And leave my one again undone, possessed.

Think not for this, however, the poor treason

Of my stout blood against my staggering brain,

I shall remember you with love, or season

My scorn with pity,—let me make it plain:

I find this frenzy insufficient reason

For conversation when we meet again.

1923

33

WOMEN

LOUISE BOGAN

Women have no wilderness in them,
They are provident instead.
Content in the tight hot cell of their hearts
To eat dusty bread.

They do not see cattle cropping red winter grass,
They do not hear
Snow water going down under culverts
Shallow and clear.

They wait, when they should turn to journeys,
They stiffen, when they should bend.
They use against themselves that benevolence
To which no man is friend.

They cannot think of so many crops to a field
Or of clean wood cleft by an axe.
Their love is an eager meaninglessness
Too tense, or too lax.

They hear in every whisper that speaks to them
A shout and a cry.
As like as not, when they take life over their door-sills
They should let it go by.

1923

STANZAS IN MEDITATION: PART FOUR, #9

GERTRUDE STEIN

How nine

Nine is not nine

Mine is not nine

Ten is not nine

Mine is not ten

Nor when

Nor which one then

Can be not then

Not only mine for ten

But any ten for which one then

I am not nine

Can be mine

Mine one at a time

Not one from nine

Nor eight at one time

For which they can be mine.

Mine is one time

As much as they know they like

I like it too to be one of one two

One two or one or two

One and one

One mine

Not one mine

And so they ask me what do I do

Can they but if they too

One is mine too

Which is one for you

Can be they like me

I like it for which they can

Not pay but say

She is not mine with not

But will they rather

Oh yes not rather not

In won in one in mine in three

In one two three

All out but me.

I find I like what I have

Very much.

1929

JESSIE MITCHELL'S MOTHER

GWENDOLYN BROOKS

Into her mother's bedroom to wash the ballooning body.

"My mother is jelly-hearted and she has a brain of jelly:

Sweet, quiver-soft, irrelevant. Not essential.

Only a habit would cry if she should die.

A pleasant sort of fool without the least iron. . . .

Are you better, mother, do you think it will come today?"

The stretched yellow rag that was Jessie Mitchell's mother

Reviewed her. Young, and so thin, and so straight.

So straight! as if nothing could ever bend her.

But poor men would bend her, and doing things with poor men,

Being much in bed, and babies would bend her over,

And the rest of things in life that were for poor women,

Coming to them grinning and pretty with intent to bend

  and to kill.

Comparisons shattered her heart, ate at her bulwarks:

The shabby and the bright: she, almost hating her daughter,

Crept into an old sly refuge: "Jessie's black

And her way will be black, and jerkier even than mine.

Mine, in fact, because I was lovely, had flowers

Tucked in the jerks, flowers were here and there. . . ."

She revived for the moment settled and dried-up triumphs,

Forced perfume into old petals, pulled up the droop,

Refueled

Triumphant long-exhaled breaths.

Her exquisitely yellow youth . . .

1960

BEARS

A D R I E N N E   R I C H

Wonderful bears that walked my room all night,
Where are you gone, your sleek and fairy fur,
Your eyes' veiled imperious light?

Brown bears as rich as mocha or as musk,
White opalescent bears whose fur stood out
Electric in the deepening dusk,

And great black bears who seemed more blue than black,
More violet than blue against the dark—
Where are you now? upon what track

Mutter your muffled paws, that used to tread
So softly, surely, up the creakless stair
While I lay listening in bed?

When did I lose you? whose have you become?
Why do I wait and wait and never hear
Your thick nocturnal pacing in my room?
My bears, who keeps you now, in pride and fear?

1955

HER KIND

ANNE SEXTON

I have gone out, a possessed witch,
haunting the black air, braver at night;
dreaming evil, I have done my hitch
over the plain houses, light by light:
lonely thing, twelve-fingered, out of mind.
A woman like that is not a woman, quite.
I have been her kind.

I have found the warm caves in the woods,
filled them with skillets, carvings, shelves,
closets, silks, innumerable goods;
fixed the suppers for the worms and the elves:
whining, rearranging the disaligned.
A woman like that is misunderstood.
I have been her kind.

I have ridden in your cart, driver,
waved my nude arms at villages going by,
learning the last bright routes, survivor
where your flames still bite my thigh
and my ribs crack where your wheels wind.
A woman like that is not ashamed to die.
I have been her kind.

1960

MORNING SONG

SYLVIA PLATH

love set you going like a fat gold watch.
the midwife slapped your footsoles, and your bald cry
took its place among the elements.

our voices echo, magnifying your arrival. new statue.
in a drafty museum, your nakedness
shadows our safety. we stand round blankly as walls.

i'm no more your mother
than the cloud that distils a mirror to reflect its own slow
effacement at the wind's hand

all night your moth-breath
flickers among the flat pink roses. i wake to listen;
a far sea moves in my ear.

one cry, and i stumble from bed, cow-heavy and floral
in my victorian nightgown.
your mouth opens clear as a cat's; the window square

whitens and swallows its dull stars. and now you try
your handful of notes;
the clear vowels rise like balloons.

1966

HOMAGE TO MY HIPS

LUCILLE CLIFTON

these hips are big hips.

they need space to

move around in.

they don't fit into little

petty places. these hips

are free hips.

they don't like to be held back.

these hips have never been enslaved,

they go where they want to go

they do what they want to do.

these hips are mighty hips.

these hips are magic hips.

i have known them

to put a spell on a man and

spin him like a top!

1980

IN COLD STORM LIGHT
LESLIE MARMON SILKO

In cold storm light
I watch the sandrock
        canyon rim.

The wind is wet
        with the smell of piñon.
The wind is cold
        with the sound of juniper.
                And then
                        out of the thick ice sky
                                running swiftly
                                pounding
                                swirling above the treetops
                        The snow elk come,
                        Moving, moving
                                white song
                                storm wind in the branches.

And when the elk have passed
        behind them
                a crystal train of snowflakes
                strands of mist
                        tangled in rocks
                        and leaves.

1981

LOST SISTER
CATHY SONG

I

In China,
even the peasants
name their first daughters
Jade—
the stone that in the far fields
could moisten the dry season,
could make men move mountains
for the healing green of the inner hills
glistening like slices of winter melon.

And the daughters were grateful:
They never left home.
To move freely was a luxury
stolen from them at birth.
Instead, they gathered patience,
learning to walk in shoes
the size of teacups.
without breaking—
the arc of their movements
as dormant as the rooted willow,
as redundant as the farmyard hens.
But they traveled far
in surviving,
learning to stretch the family rice,
to quiet the demons,
the noisy stomachs.

2

There is a sister
across the ocean,
who relinquished her name,
diluting the jade green
with the blue of the Pacific.
Rising with the tide of locusts,
She swarmed with others
to inundate another shore.
In America,
there are many roads
and women can stride along with men.

But in another wilderness,
the possibilities,
the loneliness,
can strangulate like jungle vines.
The meager provisions and sentiments
of once belonging—
fermented roots, Mah-Jong tiles and firecrackers—set but
a flimsy household
in a forest of nightless cities.
A giant snake rattles above,
spewing black clouds into your kitchen.
Dough-faced landlords
slip in and out of your keyholes,
making claims you don't understand,
tapping into your communication systems
of laundry lines and restaurant chains.

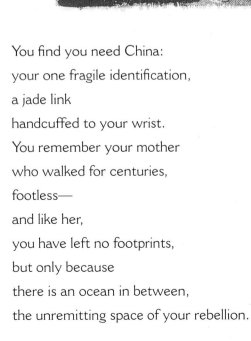

You find you need China:
your one fragile identification,
a jade link
handcuffed to your wrist.
You remember your mother
who walked for centuries,
footless—
and like her,
you have left no footprints,
but only because
there is an ocean in between,
the unremitting space of your rebellion.

1983

GOOD HOTDOGS

SANDRA CISNEROS

Fifty cents apiece

To eat our lunch

We'd run

Straight from school

Instead of home

Two blocks

Then the store

That smelled like steam

You ordered

Because you had the money

Two hotdogs and two pops for here

Everything on the hotdogs

Except pickle lily

Dash those hotdogs

Into buns and splash on

All that good stuff

Yellow mustard and onions

And french fries piled up on top all

Rolled up in a piece of wax

Paper for us to hold hot

In our hands

Quarters on the counter

Sit down

Good hotdogs

We'd eat

Fast till there was nothing left

But salt and poppy seeds even

The little burnt tips

Of french fries

We'd eat

You humming

And me swinging my legs

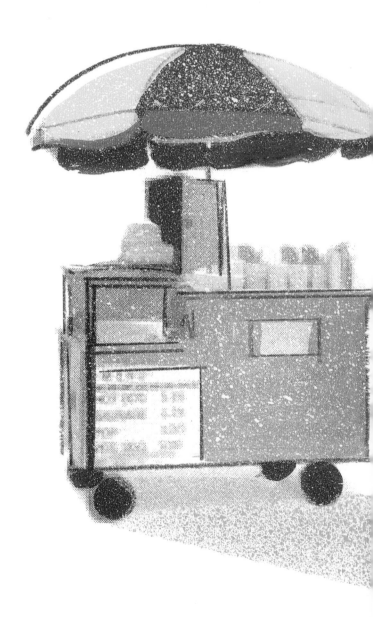

1987

WHAT DO WOMEN WANT?

MARY JO SALTER

"Look! It's a wedding!" At the ice cream shop's
pristine picture window, the fortyish
blonde in the nice-mother shorts and top
stops short to raise two cones, one in each hand,
as if to toast the frothy blur of bride
emerging from St. Brigid's across the green.
"Mom," a boy answers, "I said I wanted a *dish*."
But this washes under her, while a well-matched band
of aqua-clad attendants pours outside
to laugh among fresh, buttonholed young men.

Young men . . . remember *them*? Her entourage
now is six boys, and she buys each one his wish.
When she peers up from her purse, the newlyweds
have sped away, and she notices at last,
on the littered steps of the Universalist
Society, some ten yards from St. Brigid's,
a rat-haired old woman in a camouflage
Army-Navy outfit, in whose pockets bulge
rags, or papers, and an unbagged beverage.
Looks like a flask of vodka. But no, it's dish-

washing liquid! It's Ivory, the household god.
The shape is clear from here: a voodoo doll,
headless, with the waist pinched, like a bride.
Poor thing—her dirty secret nothing worse
than the dream of meals to wash up after. While
what *she* most craves, standing at this font
of hope, the soda-fountain, with the boys
all eating hand-to-mouth, is not to miss
the thing that . . . well, it's hard to say; but what
she'd want, if we were given what we want.

1994

THE GIRLS IN THE CIRCLE

NIKKI GIOVANNI

The girls in the circle
Have painted their toes

They twisted their braids
With big yellow bows

The took Grandma's face powder
And powdered each nose

And sprayed *Evening In Paris*
All over their clothes

They are amazed
At how they look
They smell good too
Mother may not be amused

The girls in the circle
Now tease and giggle

They look so grown up
With that high heel wiggle

Their pearls are flapping
Their dresses flow

They are so sorry
They have no place to go

Mother refuses to drive them
Anywhere
Looking like that

2003

BY ACCIDENT

JULIA ALVAREZ

Sometimes I think I became the woman
I am by accident, nothing prepared
the way, not a dramatic wayward aunt
or moody mother who read *Middlemarch,*
or godmother who whispered, You can be
whatever you want! and by doing so
performed the god-like function of breathing
grit into me. Even my own sisters
were more concerned with hairdryers and boys
than the poems I recited ad nauseum

in our shared bedrooms when the lights were out.
You're making me sick! my sisters would say
as I ranted on, Whitman's *Song of Myself*
not the best lullaby, I now admit,
or Chaucer in middle English which caused
many a nightmare fight. Mami! they'd called,
She's doing it again! Slap of slippers
in the hall, door clicks, and lights snapped on.
Why can't you be considerate for once?
"I am," I pleaded, "these are sounds, sweet airs,

that give delight and—" Keep it to yourself!
my mother said, which more than anything
anyone in my childhood advised
turned me to this paper solitude
where I both keep things secret and broadcast
my heart for all the world to read. And so,
through many drafts, I became the woman
I kept to myself as I lay awake
in that dark bedroom with the lonesome sound
of their sweet breathing as my sisters slept.

2003

A ROAD THROUGH THE WOODS
MARGE PIERCY

A road through the woods
is paved with fallen leaves
that crush beneath our soles
a ripe earthy smell, decay
and a certain toasty scent:

the road dips down, sidles
up a shallow hill to the crest
of oaks, easy to walk on
side by side, a golden road
summoning, so that we hike

miles farther than we meant to.
The woods are ours a few
weeks more before hunters come
to soak the leaves with blood.
A time to harvest butternut,

striped delicata, the grooved
Red Rouge Vif d'Estampes pumpkins,
bring in the green tomatoes
before frost softens them to rot,
season of pears laid in paper

of the first good apples hanging
bright as poppies against the wood,
season of hawks, hunting over the cliff,
on the wind, hunting over the cliff.
The swallows, warblers are gone

with the summer daisies. Crickets
chirp suddenly from under
the radiator. Spiders web
the high corners. Golden
moment that will fade quickly

to leaves the color of old blood,
to skeletal weeds, to the world
thinned down, only the birds
who winter here, only wood
and stone and monotone to see.

2003

WOMEN WHO CAME BEFORE US

NAOMI SHIHAB NYE

Our mothers stirred potatoes and herbs
in a pot on the stove. They were sniffing the air,
their deep eyes tuned. "Speak up," they sang.
"Say what you mean."

Our grandmothers hurt in their knees
and their necks. The world had not been easy for them.
Maybe no one had listened enough. My grandma whispered
in my ear, "You want that doll? You'll get that doll."

And far away the secret women,
women in cloaks, wandering stone,
sent us messages on the air.
"You're never, never ever alone."

What words would we shape?
Where could we stand?
Women always gripped my hand.
They led me through the city crowds.

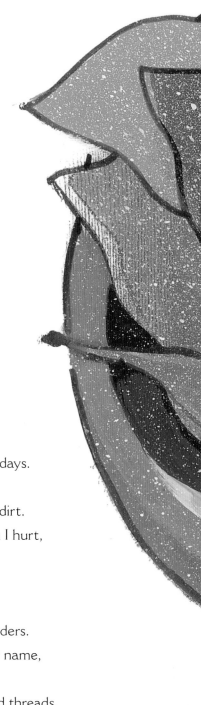

I'd pull my poem from the wool of days.
Comb its hair, sing the praise
of friends and forests, dreams and dirt.
Write when I laughed, write when I hurt,

sing when no one fit my wish.
"Nothing here is what I ordered."
Poems would take me past my borders.
Back to the women who wove my name,

the sewing basket with needles and threads,
the silver thimble, the cozy bed,
the plumped-up pillow, the hand-stitched quilt.
And what would we say? What would we say?

A poem was waiting every day.

2003

POET BIOGRAPHIES

JULIA ALVAREZ (1950–) is a true daughter of the Americas—born in Manhattan, but spending most of the first decade of her life in her parents' native country, the Dominican Republic. Politics forced her father, a doctor, to relocate his family back to New York City when Julia was ten. Because she spoke Spanish with her parents and English at school, she claimed her spoken language was "Spanglish." When she was thirteen, her parents sent her to Abbot Academy and before she finished high school, she knew she wanted to be a writer. Becoming bilingual by necessity, she commented, "I came to English late but to the profession early." Alvarez went on to Middlebury College, where she majored in literature and writing, graduating in 1971. While in college, she was required to read writers like Jane Austen and Emily Dickinson, writers she loved. But Alvarez worried that she "had to write like them in order to be a writer in English." Instead she found her own voice, and learned to create characters that reflected her own family's heritage, that reflected the lives of "women of two cultures."

In 1974, Alvarez was awarded the American Academy of Poetry Prize and the next year, she earned her MFA from Syracuse University. She published her first book of poems in 1984, and her first novel, *How the Garcia Girls Lost Their Accents*, in 1990. Married with two children, Alvarez has written several books for children, publishing in both English and Spanish. She has taught at several universities before returning to her alma mater, Middlebury, where she is a Professor of English. In 1996, her volume *Homecoming: New and Collected Poems* appeared. "By Accident" has not been previously published.

LOUISE BOGAN (1897–1970) grew up in her native Maine and was educated in private schools. She attended Boston University, but dropped out of college after only a year when she married an army officer. She gave birth to a daughter, but was widowed in 1920. The young mother spent time abroad in Vienna, Austria, and she published her first book of poetry, *Body of this Death*, in 1923. When she returned to New York City, her friend Margaret Mead helped her to get a job working at the Columbia University Library. She needed to earn a living, but poetry was her life. Bogan self-consciously turned her back on the romantic themes of Victorian women poets who came before her. In some verses, she used characters from Greek and Roman mythology, but Bogan creatively reworked these stories to compose poems that were tart and insightful. Her verse was praised for its direct, unvarnished style. In 1925, she married Raymond Holden, an editor at *The New Yorker*, and in 1931, she became the magazine's poetry editor. Shortly thereafter, she suffered a nervous breakdown and she and Holden divorced. Despite writing blocks and severe bouts of depression, Bogan continued to compose verse, and even to win prestigious prizes. In later life, she concentrated on teaching and literary criticism. Many of her poems wove sharp social commentary into her spare, graceful lines. She died of a heart attack in 1970.

ANNE BRADSTREET (1612–1672), the well-educated daughter of Lincoln-shire Puritans, set sail from England to Massachusetts with her husband when she was only eighteen. She described: "I found a new world and new manners, at which my heart rose. . . ."

In 1630, Bradstreet began her new life in the Massachusetts Bay Colony at the center of her growing household. She would eventually give birth to eight children—moving from a home in Cambridge, then to Ipswich, and finally, in 1644, to the remote settlement of North Andover. Although her father would become governor of the colony and Bradstreet was a member of the Puritan elite, this did not help the isolated wife and mother with her struggles on the frontier.

She poured emotions into her writing, sharing verses only with her family until 1650, when, without her knowledge, her brother-in-law had a selection of her poems published in England, *The Tenth Muse Lately Sprung Up in America*. As her literary "descendant," contemporary poet Adrienne Rich observes: "To have written these, the first good poems in America while rearing eight children; lying frequently sick, keeping house at the edge of wilderness was to have managed a poet's range and extension within confines as severe as any American poet has confronted." Bradstreet transformed challenges within her own life—such as the burning of her home in 1666—into subjects for her verses. Bradstreet also made the images and metaphors of a woman's life the creative force from which her poetry sprang.

GWENDOLYN BROOKS (1917–2000) was born in Kansas, but called Chicago home, as she moved there with her parents when she was just a toddler. Growing up on Chicago's South Side, in a neighborhood known as Bronzeville, the budding writer filled notebook after notebook with her compositions. By the age of thirteen, Brook published her first poem. She graduated from Englewood High School, and then earned her degree from Wilson Junior College in 1936. Her writing began to appear in anthologies, and she became a contributor to a radical newspaper, the *Chicago Defender*. In 1939, she married writer Henry Blakely and the couple had two children. Langston Hughes encouraged Brooks to continue her writing. In 1943, she won an award from the Midwestern Writers Conference. In 1945, she published her first collection of poems, *A Street in Bronzeville*, which garnered her praise and attention: *Mademoiselle* named her as one of its ten Women of the Year. Her second volume, *Annie Allen*, won the Pulitzer Prize for Poetry in 1950, making Brooks the first African-American to receive this award. She accepted teaching positions—at the University of Wisconsin, at Northeastern Illinois University, at Columbia University—but she always returned home to her beloved Chicago. The Black Arts movement of the 1960s (the artistic sister of the Black Power Movement) had a very great impact on her writing. Also her poetry continues to influence a new generation of black writers such as Rita Dove who praised her "lifewords that nourished like meat, not frosting." In 1968, she succeeded Carl Sandburg as the Poet Laureate of Illinois and in 1976, was the first African-American to receive an American Academy of Arts and Letters Award. She not only published over twenty volumes of verse, but Brooks also led workshops to encourage young blacks to find their voices through poetry, even sponsoring programs in neighborhoods dominated by gangs. Until her death from cancer in 2000, Brooks was committed to bringing poetry to the people.

LYDIA MARIA CHILD (1802–1880) was the youngest of six children born into a family in Medford, Massachusetts. She spent most of her life fighting for the rights of others—for American Indians to be treated fairly, for slaves to be emancipated. She wanted to write to advance reform. As a girl of New England, she was given only a basic education before beginning her career as a schoolteacher. Interested in creative expression, she wrote her first novel at the age of twenty-two. Then she founded a children's magazine, *Juvenile Miscellany*, in 1826. She married David Child, a committed abolitionist, in 1828. For a number of years, she made a success of publishing how-to books for homemakers and biographies of famous women. This won her a wide and loyal readership by 1830. But when she converted to the anti-slavery cause and wrote *An Appeal in Favor of that Class of Americans Called Africans* (1833), this put an end to her popularity as a children's writer. Her strong political stand against slavery was considered extreme and "unladylike" and her magazine folded. Child went on writing poetry and publishing fiction for children throughout the 1840s and into the 1850s. She is best known today as one of a group of influential women reformers of the nineteenth century whose political writings were ahead of their time. Yet some of her verses for children—set to music—remain beloved and live on.

SANDRA CISNEROS (1954–) is the daughter of a Mexican father and a Chicana mother, the only daughter of seven children in her family. Many of her early poems deal with her sense of isolation, and in one poem, "Six Brothers," she reworks the Brothers Grimms's fairy tale of six swans. During girlhood, she loved to escape into the world of books. Her family traveled between Mexico City and Chicago as she was growing up, so she learned to negotiate two cultures—the Hispanic heritage of her family and the English-speaking culture in which she needed to succeed. In her Chicago high school, Cisneros became the editor of its literary magazine and went on to earn her degree from Loyola College. Then she taught high school English in the Chicago barrios before going to the University of Iowa where she earned an MA in the school's acclaimed writing program. In 1980, she published her first book of poetry and in 1984, her first novel appeared. Much of Cisneros's work celebrates "wild women" and reflects her own free spirit. In one of her poems, "Old Maids," she describes the women of her family who cross-examine her about why she has no husband, but reminds her readers of "Señora Pumpkin Shell" (the wife of Peter-Peter Pumpkin Eater, of nursery tale fame, who gets locked away by her husband). Her powerful voice has won her a wide audience, and she earned the prestigious MacArthur Award in 1995, the very same year her collection of poems, *Loose Woman*, was re-issued. Many of her verses are full of earthy and personal themes, as in "Down There" where words "snapped like bra straps." Cisneros makes her home in San Antonio, Texas, where she works with students at a local arts center, and volunteers her talents for activist projects. She lives in a big purple house filled with cats, dogs, and parrots—and poetry.

LUCILLE CLIFTON (1936–) when she was young loved the poems her mother would read to her—some of which Lucille's own mother had written. Clifton wanted to write poetry, too, but as an African-American, she confessed, "One never saw a person who looked like me as a published poet. I certainly didn't in the schools in Buffalo [New York] where I grew up." Her father was a steelworker and her mother worked in a laundry, but they sent their six-teen-year-old daughter to Howard University. After two years, she transferred to Fredonia State Teacher's College, graduating in 1955.

Although Clifton worked in clerical jobs in Washington, D.C. to support herself, her true vocation was poetry. She sent poems to black poet Robert Hayden, who had them entered into a contest in 1969. After her writing won her a YM-YWHA Poetry Center Discovery Award, Clifton published her first book, *Good Times* (1969), named one of the year's ten best by *The New York Times*. She moved to Maryland to become a poet in residence at Coppin State College. A quilter, Clifton feels deeply indebted to her African ancestors, which she explored in her memoir: *Generations*. In much of her writing, this prolific mother of six emphasizes the importance of family. She has published over a dozen children's books, as well as several poetry collections.

From 1979 to 1982, Clifton was the Poet Laureate of Maryland where she now resides, and remains a professor at St. Mary's College in Maryland. She explains, "My students inspire me. They keep me young, keep me wanting to know what's going on in the world." A collection of her poetry, *Blessing the Boats: New and Selected Poems, 1988–2000* was published in 2001.

EMILY DICKINSON (1830–1886), an eccentric and mysterious celebrity in her native Amherst, Massachusetts, remains one of the most enigmatic literary personalities of the nineteenth century. The shy, introverted poet was born into a distinguished New England family. Although she spent time with her older brother and younger sister while growing up, Dickinson's penchant for solitude was not discouraged by her aloof father and invalid mother. She attended Amherst Academy but dropped out of college at nearby Mt. Holyoke after only a year. She kept up a steady stream of correspondence with friends and family, but increasingly cut herself off from society.

Dickinson decorated her room with portraits of favorite writers like George Eliot and Elizabeth Barrett Browning. Some scholars suggest her solitary life was the result of a "disappointment in love," but members of her family claimed that Dickinson simply embraced the world she created for herself, choosing seclusion over company. The withdrawn young woman wore only white and chose not to leave her father's yard, even withdrawing when guests appeared at the house. Poems became her companions, and Dickinson enclosed verses in letters to friends. She even struck up a correspondence in the 1860s with Thomas Wentworth Higginson, the editor of *The Atlantic Monthly*, the leading journal of its day. Higginson encouraged Dickinson, praised her talent, and even visited the reclusive poet in 1870. Despite her talent and connections, Dickinson only published eight poems during her lifetime. Her indifference to punctuation, grammar, and even rhyme, as well as her curious rhythms and broken meters made Dickinson's verses unique. It was only after her death in 1886 that nearly a thousand other verses were discovered, hidden away in her room. The fact that Dickinson's gifts were so shrouded during her lifetime has added to the fascination surrounding her literary reputation. Both her poetry and her life have provided inspiration for generations after.

ALICE DUNBAR-NELSON (1875–1935) was born the daughter of black middle-class parents in New Orleans, and graduated from Straight College (which later became Dillard University). Like many young black women of her class and generation, she became a teacher. She also wrote poetry and began to publish her verses, even in the prestigious *Boston*

Monthly Review. One of her poems and an accompanying photograph caught the attention of a rising black literary star, Paul Laurence Dunbar. He began a correspondence with the aspiring young woman poet, and romance blossomed. Although her family raised objections, she married Dunbar in 1889. After the wedding, Alice earned a master's degree at Cornell University. But the union was plagued by Paul's alcoholism and subsequent domestic violence—which led to the break-up of the marriage. It was an uphill battle, trying to extract herself from her abusive marriage, while trying to establish herself as a writer. Yet Nelson managed to publish her first book, *Violets and other Tales* (1895), followed by *Goodness of St. Rocque* (1899). Her verses reflected her commitment to racial justice, to women's equality and other important issues of the day. Nelson earned her living by teaching school in New York City. She was invited to become head of Howard High School in Wilmington, Delaware—a post she held for eighteen years. In 1916, she married journalist Robert Nelson, editor of *The Wilmington Advocate*, where she became an associate editor. While a columnist for the paper, she saw her writing career flourish—publishing plays, short stories, and, of course, poetry until her death in 1935.

NIKKI GIOVANNI (1943–) was born in Knoxville and moved to Cincinnati with her parents when just a young girl. But the black teenager later returned to Tennessee to live with her grandmother and finish high school. Then she went on to Fisk University, a traditionally all-black college, where she became involved in political and literary movements. She attended graduate school at both the University of Pennsylvania and Columbia University, where writing remained her primary passion. As a member of the Black Arts movement (the artistic sister of the Black Power Movement), Giovanni not only composed original verse, but also recorded poems set to music, sometimes with gospel accompaniment. In 1967, Giovanni published her first volume of poetry, *Black Feeling*. As the title of her first book indicated, Giovanni was part of the young, radical generation of African- American writers who directly challenged the white establishment. They followed a different drummer, one that danced to African as well as European rhythms. Giovanni was also committed, as a single mother, to producing books for children. She has remained a popular and prolific writer for more than three decades; she has more than two dozen books in print. Giovanni teaches English at Virginia Tech, and has received both the Langston Hughes Medal for Poetry and an N.A.A.C.P. Image Award.

A collection of new poems, *Blues: For All the Changes*, appeared in 1999. "The Girls in the Circle" has not been previously published.

JULIA WARD HOWE (1819–1910) was born into a wealthy New York family and was married, at the age of twenty-one, to a man twice her age, Massachusetts educator Samuel Ward Howe. The young bride settled into a conventional routine as a housewife in Boston and eventually became the mother of six. She was known to her circle of Boston intellectuals as a bright young matron who had aspirations beyond household responsibilities. Howe began to compose poems and share them with her friends—and eventually published a book of verse, *Passion Flowers*, in 1854. Unfortunately, Howe's husband disapproved of his wife's poetry—especially some of the themes of love and betrayal she explored in her verses. He belittled her accomplishments, although she drew praise from fellow Bostonians. This friction drove a wedge between the couple. Regardless, Howe continued to write, publishing a second book, *Words for the Hour*, in 1857. By the time of the Civil War, she had gained a strong following among New England readers. During the war, her patriotic verses became celebrated—and became her most enduring legacy. One of her poems, when set to music, became a favorite of both Yankee soldiers and the northern homefront: "The Battle-Hymn of the Republic." Lincoln reportedly wept when he first heard the song, and Howe became a celebrity overnight. After the war, Howe chose to live apart from her husband and poured her energies into writing and lecturing. Wherever she went, Howe was best remembered for her stirring wartime lyrics. Four thousand sang "The Battle-Hymn of the Republic" at her 1910 memorial service in Boston's Symphony Hall. She is buried in Mt. Auburn Cemetery, in Cambridge, Massachusetts, next to her husband, with whom she eventually reconciled.

LUCY LARCOM (1824–1893) enjoyed an idyllic girlhood in a Massachusetts seaport until her father died in 1833. She then accompanied her mother and siblings to the factory town of Lowell where she began to work in the cotton mills at age eleven. She changed bobbins on a spinning frame from five in the morning until seven at night. But within five years she had worked her way up in the factory system to become a bookkeeper, which gave her more time for her interest in writing. Larcom was a poet and interested in finding outlets for her creativity. She and her sister Emmeline created a magazine for the mills girls to publish poems and other pieces of writing. By 1842, the magazine merged with *The Lowell Offering*, and was reaching nearly four thousand subscribers. Larcom left the mills to pursue her education and eventually became a teacher herself. She published her first collection of verse in 1868, a volume entitled *Poems*. Throughout her long and productive literary career, she encouraged other young women to obtain an education and find a rewarding vocation, as she had. Many of her poems were didactic, intended to convey a moral to the reader. And a large number of her verses reflected the simple pleasures of everyday life, featuring poetic attempts to recapture the idyllic girlhood left behind.

EMMA LAZARUS (1849–1887) was born into a wealthy family of New York German Jews. The shy young girl translated German poems into English, before she went on to compose her own verses. At the age of seventeen, she published her first book: *Poems and Translations* (1867). After she met Ralph Waldo Emerson, he encouraged her poetry writing and became her mentor. Lazarus dedicated her next book of verses, *Admetus and other Poems* (1871), to him. The assassination of Alexander II of Russia stimulated political persecutions and eventually resulted in pogroms (forced removals) of Eastern European Jews from their homes. In response, Lazarus wrote political verses, such as "Dance of Death," a celebration of Jewish heroism, included in her next collection, *Songs of a Semite* (1882). Her most famous poem, "The New Colossus," written for a charity auction in 1883, described refugees seeking a new home in America. She became celebrated when her words were carved onto the base of the newly erected Statue of Liberty in New York City's harbor. She embraced this literary fame and fulfilled a lifelong dream of a trip to Europe, where she was welcomed by fellow poet Robert Browning and other luminaries. Struck down by cancer, Lazarus died in 1887, the same year that her final book appeared, *By the Waters of Babylon*.

EDNA ST. VINCENT MILLAY (1892–1950) was pushed by her mother to let her talents shine when she was growing up in Maine. At the age of twenty, she composed a poem which won her a national contest. Following this triumph, "Vincent," as she was known to friends and family, earned a scholarship to Vassar College. After graduation, she decided to pursue a bohemian life as a writer in New York City. Writing for the magazine *Vanity Fair* and penning plays for the Provincetown Players, Millay gathered a wide circle of admirers, including Edmund Wilson, an influential literary critic (who asked her to marry him and was turned down). Wilson explained that Millay had "an intoxicating effect on people." Her poems departed dramatically from traditional literary fare and she was hailed as the embodiment of "The New Woman." Awarded the Pulitzer Prize for Poetry in 1923 for *The Harp Weaver*, Millay became the first woman to win this prestigious honor. Her marriage to a wealthy businessman, willing to cater to his wife's free spirit and unconventional views, allowed Millay to use her celebrity status to promote political protests, including the fight against Fascism in the 1930s. In

1944, she suffered a nervous breakdown, and in 1949, she was left alone when her husband died at their rural New York home, Steepletop. Before her death in 1950, Millay was the most famous woman poet of her generation.

MARIANNE MOORE (1887–1972) grew up in awe of her mother, who took a teaching job and raised a son and daughter after her husband abandoned the family. Moore attended Bryn Mawr College where she submitted poems to her college literary magazine. She returned home to Carlisle, Pennsylvania, until she and her mother moved, first to Princeton to be near her brother, and then to Greenwich Village in New York City. A librarian by day, Moore spent her evenings among the literati, befriended by Wallace Stevens and other established poets who recognized this young woman's talents and rekindled her interest in writing. Her poems appeared first in literary magazines, then, in 1921, she published her first collection. By the time of her second book of poems in 1924, *Observations*, Moore was a celebrated figure. She became editor of a New York literary journal, *The Dial*, from 1925 until its demise in 1929. That year Moore moved with her mother and brother to a home in Brooklyn, where she became a frequent fan at Brooklyn Dodger baseball games—wearing her trademark tri-cornered hat and black cloak to games. She most often wrote at a desk, but when in the middle of a composition, Moore might keep the half-finished poem on a clipboard with her "even when I'm dusting or washing the dishes." A visitor to her apartment reported she kept a bushel basket in which to throw away drafts of compositions that weren't good enough, as she was such a perfectionist. Her slim volumes of poetry appeared with regularity and won her numerous honors, including the National Book Award and Pulitzer Prize. T.S. Eliot praised Moore's "gift for detailed observation." She was an eccentric and beloved figure among her circle of New York writers, dubbed "our saint," by William Carlos Williams.

NAOMI SHIHAB NYE (1952–) grew up in St. Louis with an American-born mother and a Palestinian father. She started composing verse from the age of six, and recalled, "I liked the portable, comfortable shape of poems. I like the space around them and the way you hold their words at arm's length and look at them. And especially the way they took you to a deeper, quieter place." As a young girl, she was especially grateful for close family ties.

She enjoyed the stories told by both of her grandmothers—one of whom was Palestinian and the other who was German. At the age of seven, Naomi published her first poem. At the age of fourteen, she moved to Jerusalem with her family where she attended high school. Her interest in writing continued and Nye saw her work appear in magazines such as *Seventeen*, and journals such as *Ironweed* and *Modern Poetry Studies*. She received her BA from Trinity University in 1974, and now lives with her husband and son in San Antonio, Texas. She is a fan of travel, and is one of the few people she knows who loves being in airports—where she can both read and write. She advises all young poets to create "a writing circle," to find a few people to share and discuss compositions, because a writer needs to create a support system. Her first book of poetry, *Different Ways to Pray*, appeared in 1980. A new collection, *19 Varieties of Gazelle*, appeared in 2002. "The Women Who Came Before Us" has not been previously published.

MARGE PIERCY (1936–), raised in a working-class neighborhood in Detroit, was the first member of her family to go to college. She won a writing scholarship to attend the University of Michigan and went on to graduate school at Northwestern, earning her MA in 1958. While trying to become a published writer in Chicago during the 1960s, she took a series of jobs to support herself: secretary, switchboard operator, department store clerk, and artist's model. She became involved in both the civil rights movement and the growing protest movement against America's military involvement in Vietnam. Throughout this period, she was struggling to earn a living as a writer—in Boston, San Francisco, Ann Arbor, and Brooklyn. Working as a political organizer in New York, her failing health and the uphill battle of radical politics left her drained. She relocated to Cape Cod, Massachusetts, where she learned to enjoy gardening, the company of cats, and the extended community of the Boston women's movement. She and her husband, Ira Wood, are cofounders of the Leapfrog Press. Her frank and direct portraits of women's issues have earned her praise as a "poet of womanhood and compassion, conscience and spirit, and her poems are as magnetic as mirrors." Piercy gives readings and workshops around the world, and tells her audience: "Some poems are a journey of discovering and exploration for the writer as well as the reader. I find out where I am going when I finally arrive, which may take years." She takes extreme pleasure in the act of writing and suggests, "You can turn a poem round and about and upside down, dancing with a kind of bolero of two snakes twisting and coiling, until the poem has found its right and proper shape." She remains committed to a variety of political causes and movements for spiritual renewal. A book of verse, *The Art of Blessing the Day*, was published in 2000. "A Road Through the Woods" has not been previously published.

SYLVIA PLATH (1932–1963) was the only child of immigrant parents: her father left Poland for America and became a biologist at Boston University, while her German-born mother taught English in a local high school. Following her father's death, Plath at the age of eight began to write poetry to escape the unhappiness caused by this loss. Her poems had a stark, melancholy undertone. Her talents won her a scholarship to Smith College in 1950. She was named a guest editor of *Mademoiselle*, after she won the magazine's coveted college fiction prize. During this period, Plath's psychological problems began to emerge. Following a suicide attempt, she dropped out of college, but returned to graduate in 1955. Plath went abroad to England to study at Cambridge University where she met poet Ted Hughes. Shortly thereafter, the couple married. She returned to the United States to take a teaching position in the English Department at Smith College. However, Plath soon gave it up to write full-time, and lived in Boston, studying with poet Robert Lowell. She complained that "inhibition" was keeping her from writing what she really felt. In 1959, Plath and Hughes decided to settle in England. They lived in rural Devon where Plath gave birth to a daughter in 1960. In 1961, she suffered a miscarriage, underwent an appendectomy, and suffered increasingly poor health, but gave birth to a son in 1962. During this challenging period, Plath published two books of verse—*The Colossus* (1960) and *Three Women: A Monologue for Three Voices* (1962). Her poems were full of brooding intensity, and she joined the ranks of "confessional poets." When Hughes became involved with another woman, the young mother took her two children and went to live alone in London. The winter of 1962–63 was bitterly cold, and Plath and her children often fell ill. Crushed by self-doubts and financial worries, she slowly sank into despair. Plath claimed she was writing her best poems ever, and her autobiographical novel, *The Bell Jar*, appeared (under a pseudonym) in January 1963. But even this accomplishment could not stave off the thirty-one-year-old poet's sense of impending doom. In February, 1963, Plath committed suicide. Several volumes of poetry appeared posthumously—including her best-selling *Ariel* (1965), *Crossing the Water* (1971), and a volume of *Collected Poems* (1981), which won the Pulitzer Prize. Plath's work and career remain the subject of popular interest and scholarly study, and she remains one of the most celebrated women poets of the twentieth century.

ADRIENNE RICH (1929–) grew up in a comfortable middle-class family in Baltimore, where her father was a physician and professor at Johns Hopkins University. Her mother had given up a promising musical career to raise her two daughters. Her parents were fiercely ambitious for their daughter, who graduated from Radcliffe College with honors. A *Change of World*, her first book of poems, appeared in 1951, and won the Yale Younger Poets

Award. In 1953, she married a Harvard economist and had three children before the age of thirty; by 1960, the pressures of family life filled her with "despair at my own failures, despair, too, at my fate . . . ." In 1966, the couple and their three sons moved to New York City, where Rich was hired to be an adjunct faculty member at Columbia University, and found a creative outlet through teaching and publishing. As volumes of poetry and prose appeared with regularity, her reputation grew. Her fellow poet W.S. Merwin praises: "All of her life, she has been in love with the hope of telling the utter truth, and her command of language from the first has been startlingly powerful." She became increasingly involved in radical politics, most especially the women's movement. Widowed in 1970, Rich continued writing and teaching. When her volume of verse, *Diving Into the Wreck*, won the National Book Award in 1974, Rich accepted "in the name of all women who are silenced." She is passionately committed to her art: "Poetry is liberative language, connecting the fragments within us, connecting us to others like and unlike ourselves, replenishing our desire." Rich is actively involved in campaigns for gay and lesbian civil liberties. A recipient of the prestigious MacArthur Award, she now lives in California. A collection of her poems entitled *Fox* appeared in 2001.

MARY JO SALTER (1954–) was born in Grand Rapids, Michigan, and attended Harvard University where she studied with poets Robert Fitzgerald and Elizabeth Bishop. She went on to study at Cambridge University in England. Salter has traveled to Japan, Iceland, and spent a year in France on an Amy Lowell Poetry Travelling Fellowship. She currently "job-shares" a teaching position in the Department of English at Mt. Holyoke College with her husband, fellow poet and writer Brad Leithauser. The couple live in South Hadley, Massachusetts, and have two daughters. Salter's first poetry collection, *Henry Purcell in Japan* appeared in 1985. Her second book of verse, *Unfinished Painting*, won the 1989 Lamont Selection for the year's most distinguished second volume of poetry. This volume included a piece in honor of Emily Dickinson, an homage which followed Salter's inspirational visit to the poet's home in nearby Amherst. One critic praises Salter's "breathtaking elegance" and "intellectual subtlety," as she tackles topics which reflect an audacious range of literary and historical references. Her appreciation of both the past and the future is reflected in an address she delivered to the Mt. Holyoke Class of 2000: "In a hundred years, thanks to advances in medicine, some of you may be reasonably spry, mentally active at 122...To a greater degree than any generation in the history of the world, you will believe in the presence of the past—because you were there." Salter published a collection of poems, *Open Shutters*, in 2003.

ANNE SEXTON (1928–1974) enjoyed seaside summers in Maine when she was a young child growing up in Massachusetts. But she nevertheless had a troubled childhood and suffered from emotional problems from an early age. In 1948, she dropped out of college to marry Alfred Sexton. She gave birth to two daughters in rapid succession, and then suffered a series of nervous breakdowns. One of her doctors suggested that she enroll in a poetry course, which led to the publication of her first collection, *To Bedlam and Part Way Back* (1960). She took courses with Robert Lowell and found poetry allowed her to counter self-destructive urges, which she called her "demons." Her work allowed her to "sing in celebration of the woman I am." Her volume, *Live or Die* (1966), earned her the Pulitzer Prize. Despite this acclaim, Sexton struggled with deep psychological problems and in a very public way as her poems were full of her struggles and pain. Her writings marked her as one of the most prominent of "contemporary confessional poets." Some of the topics she tackled were extremely controversial, such as incest and drug addiction—not conventional subjects for women poets. Her groundbreaking verses were testaments to her courage. Although committed to her art, she fought depression in her private life. Sexton became increasingly dependent on alcohol and medication. She began to teach in 1970, and became a passionate advocate of poetry workshops, to which she contributed tirelessly in an effort to promote younger voices. In 1974, a month before her forty-sixth birthday, she took her own life.

LESLIE MARMON SILKO (1948–) was born in Albuquerque, New Mexico, and attended a Bureau of Indian Affairs school on the Laguna Pueblo, where she was raised. As a child of European, Mexican, and Native American ancestry, Silko keenly felt her mixed heritage. She is part of a growing group of American writers who spring from cultures that are not just different, but cultures that historically have been in conflict with one another. This made it challenging to a young girl like Leslie growing up in the American Southwest during the second half of the twentieth century.

She graduated from a Catholic high school before going on to earn her degree in English from the University of New Mexico in 1969. She attended law school, but dropped out to do graduate work in English. Silko returned to her roots and taught at a Navajo community college in Arizona. Then she spent time in Alaska. In 1974, she published her first collection of poems, *Laguna Woman*. She knew that her poems in English might build a bridge of understanding between Native Americans and readers of English poetry. Her ability to shift between these competing worlds provides a unique window, a point of entry between natives and immigrants on the continent. The role of the land and the role of storytelling within Native American cultures are key to appreciation of Silko's poetry.

She has won the Pushcart Prize, and also been awarded the prestigious MacArthur Foundation Fellowship. The divorced mother of two now teaches at the University of Arizona, and has published several acclaimed novels in the past decade.

CATHY SONG (1955–) was born in Honolulu and became fascinated from an early age by the story of her grandparents. Her grandfather was a Chinese-born laborer whose wife came from Korea as a "picture bride"—a woman who emigrated to marry a man she had never met before. Song wrote poetry while still in high school—and continued her literary interests while she attended Wellesley College, graduating in 1973. She earned a master's degree from Boston University before returning to Honolulu in 1981. The following year her first collection of poetry was published, *Picture Bride* (1982), which won her the Yale Younger Poets Award. Many of her poems are extended explorations of her family. Part of a post-World War II group of American poets who sought to change the face of American literature, Song and her generation have stimulated a popular embrace of poetry with the diversity of their styles, approaches, and voices. Their distinctive agenda has redefined American poetry. Song's intensity and quiet resolve shine through, as her verses reveal "the mind in the diamond pinpoint light of concentration tunneling into memory, released by the imagination." Song still lives and writes in Hawaii, where she is married to a physician and raising her three children. She has won the Shelley Memorial Award from the Poetry Society of America and a Pushcart Prize. Her most recent collection of poetry is *The Land of Bliss* (2001).

GERTRUDE STEIN (1874–1946) was born into an extremely intellectual Jewish immigrant family. Her Bavarian-born father taught Gertrude his native German tongue as well as French when she was just a young child growing up in California. Gertrude and her brother Leo moved to Baltimore to be raised by an aunt, following the death of their parents. The values of accomplishment and intellect continued to be emphasized within the Stein family. After attending Radcliffe College, Gertrude went back to Baltimore to Johns Hopkins University to study medicine in 1897. But she abandoned these plans and in 1903 followed her brother Leo to Paris. While living in France, Gertrude Stein was fascinated by the Impressionists (as a group of modern painters were called) who were innovative and breaking with the artistic tradition. She said she wanted to try to use "language" the way they used paint—in a breathtaking and bold fashion. In 1907, she formed what would become a lifelong partnership with fellow American-in-exile, Alice B. Toklas. In their Paris home, visiting Americans might meet artists and writers from all over the world. Stein's Paris salon (the main public room in a home) became a center for the avant-garde—artists who turned their backs on convention to pioneer new forms of creative expression. Gertrude Stein became the most famous experimental woman poet of her day. She was also one of the most prolific female writers, publishing plays, operas, novels, non-fiction, memoir, and volumes of poetry. Her poetry was groundbreaking in its disregard for traditional literary forms. She spent the remainder of her life in Paris, though forced to evacuate her home during both World War I and World War II. Her final resting place was back in her beloved Paris following her death in 1946.

PHILLIS WHEATLEY (CIRCA 1753–1784) was stolen from her native Senegambia and sold as an African slave in Boston in 1760. The seven-year-old girl was given the name Phillis, after the ship she arrived on. Her mistress, Susannah Wheatley, encouraged the bright and sensitive child who rapidly learned English, followed by Latin and Greek. She wrote verse, and in 1767, her first poem was published in a Rhode Island paper. In the spring of 1773, Wheatley accompanied her master's son to England. While in London, the Countess of Huntington became a patron, helping the young writer to publish a book of her verse. She returned to Boston and her *Poems on Various Subjects Religious and Moral* was published to great fanfare. Shortly thereafter, Wheatley was freed, but she remained with the Wheatley family until her former master died in 1778. Subsequently, she married John Peters. During the next five years, she bore three children, but did not publish any poems. But in 1784, several of her verses, including a tribute to the American Revolution, appeared in print. Despite this literary output, her fortunes were failing. Two of her children had died and her husband was imprisoned for debt. Wheatley was forced to earn a living for herself and her surviving child working in a boarding house. She had optimistically advertised her second volume of poems but died in 1784 before its completion. Despite her remarkable early fame and promise, this poet's passing was a sad and lonely demise. Nevertheless, many young African-American women honored her heroic literary gifts when they formed Phillis Wheatley Societies at the end of the nineteenth century. The spread of these clubs continued well into the twentieth century, standing as tribute to Wheatley's remarkable accomplishments.

AUTHOR'S NOTE

When I spent a lovely winter's afternoon nearly a decade ago in Stephen Alcorn's Cambridge studio, I knew I wanted his passion and vision on the pages of my books for children. I am even more grateful for his beautiful and sensitive illustrations on this, our second collaboration. My sons and his daughters have grown up in homes filled with art and poetry, and we wish it for all our children. We both believe in the vibrant voices showcased in this collection and know that they are for readers of both genders, readers of all ages — for any and all who can appreciate poetry. Read or spoken, memorized or mesmerized, we believe in poetry and know the stories, verses, and images within *A Poem of Her Own* offer something for everyone. In celebrating poets past and present, it remains my continuing goal that we will inspire a future generation to create poems of their own.

ILLUSTRATOR'S NOTE

The illustration of poetry affords me a special freedom as an artist. Poems are not always linear in their progression, and often they can transcend, quite mysteriously, our notions of space and time. As a result, when I illustrate a poem, I rarely feel the need to literally translate a given passage of text. Rather, I am moved to think metaphorically and to explore the many ways in which I might subtly compliment, or echo, if you will, not just the overriding theme of the text, but its underlying rhythm as well. Just as a poet juxtaposes words and sounds and meanings and devises rhymes that effectively rhythmically tie a poem together, I construct my pictures with an equally varied array of pictorial tools, including, but not limited to, the juxtaposition of light and shadow, straight and curved lines, positive (filled) space and negative (empty) space — and set about arranging each element so that they relate to one another on a multitude of levels, like words in a poem.

For Virginia Meacham Gould
C.C.

＋·╫═╪●D●C●┣╍·＋

To the memory of Kathleen Hornby,
a friend I found too late and lost too soon
S.A.

Designer: Allison Henry
Production Manager: Hope Koturo

The illustrations were painted directly on acid-free paper, using
light-fast casein paints, and without the aid of preliminary sketches.

Library of Congress Cataloging-in-Publication Data
A poem of her own : voices of American women yesterday and today /
edited by Catherine Clinton; illustrated by Stephen Alcorn.
     p. cm.
Summary: Presents a collection of more than 20 poems by
American women published between 1678 to 2001.
     ISBN 0-8109-4240-2
     1. Children's poetry, American—Women authors. 2. Women—United
States—Juvenile poetry. [1. American poetry. 2. Women—Poetry.]
I.Clinton, Catherine, 1952- II. Alcorn, Stephen, ill.

PS589 .P635 2003
811.008'09287— dc21

                                        2002012851

Introduction and biographies copyright © 2003 Catherine Clinton
Illustrations copyright © 2003 Stephen Alcorn

Printed and bound in China
10 9 8 7 6 5 4 3 2 1

Harry N. Abrams, Inc.
100 Fifth Avenue
New York, N.Y. 10011
www.abramsbooks.com

Abrams is a subsidiary of
LA MARTINIÈRE
GROUPE